Bala Kids
An imprint of Shambhala Publications, Inc.
2129 13th Street
Boulder, Colorado 80302
www.shambhala.com

Cover art: Aki
Cover design: Kara Plikaitis
Interior design: Kara Plikaitis

9 8 7 6 5 4 3 2 1

First Edition
Printed in Malaysia

Bala Kids makes every effort to print on acid-free, recycled paper.
Bala Kids is distributed worldwide by Penguin Random House, Inc.,
and its subsidiaries.

ISBN: 978-1-64547-082-3

Cataloging-in-Publication data is available from the Library of Congress.

THE VIBES BOOK

Hannah Clarke

Illustrated by Aki

bala kids

Vibes are a special kind of energy.

You can't see them, but you can feel them in
your body and all around you.

They're like magical, invisible feelings and thoughts.
You have to imagine what they look like.

There are lots of different kinds.

But the vibes that work the most magic are good vibes.

You can tell if someone has good vibes. They often seem happy and warm, and you always feel better when you're around them.

When you feel calm and peaceful or bursting with joy, it's usually a sign that you've got some good vibes.

You can send vibes to other people . . . and
other people can send vibes back to you.

You can send good vibes to anyone!
You can even send them all around the world.

It's easy. All you have to do is think about somebody and imagine all your lovely thoughts and energy surrounding them.

The vibes will flow from you to the person you are thinking of.

When you send someone
your good vibes, it means
you want the best for them.

If you know someone who is feeling down, you can send them some good vibes to help cheer them up.

Try not to send out bad vibes. The person you are sending them to won't feel very good—and neither will you.

But it feels great to share some good vibes!

When you send out good vibes, you'll notice that
something amazing happens: you always get them back.

And the more good vibes there are in the world,
the better everyone feels.

So start to notice the magical
energy that is always around you.

Feel the vibes and send them
out with love!

Give it a try!

A great time to start is right now.

Author's Note

This book came as a result of my kids asking me: "What ARE vibes, Mum?" I searched for a book that would help explain the concept—but I couldn't find one anywhere. So I decided to write one myself.

I do believe that the energy we send out into the world is the energy we get back. This is a simple idea, but it can really have a big impact on your life. I think it's an important message to share.